Let's Build
an Invention

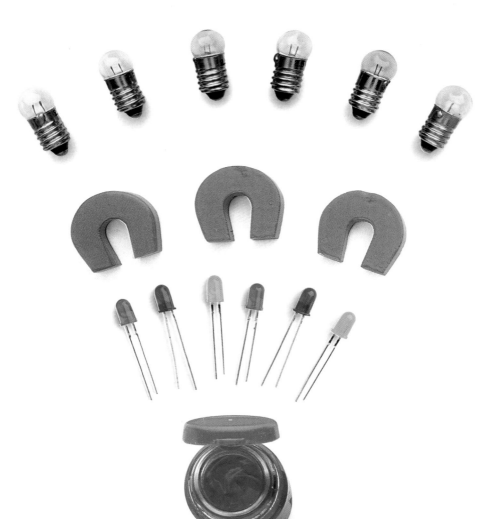

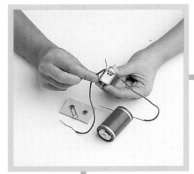

Let's Build
an Invention

JACK CHALLONER, DAVE KING,
and ANGELA WILKES

DK

How to use this book

Let's Build an Invention is full of exciting projects to do at home that will help you find out more about cameras, electricity, and how things work. Below are some points to look for on each page when using this book, and a list of things to remember.

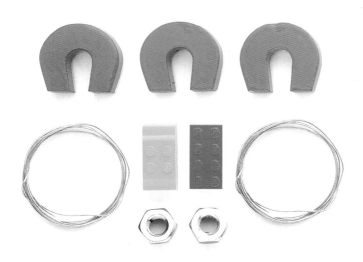

Equipment
Illustrated checklists show you which tools to have ready before you start a project.

The things you need
The items for each project are clearly shown to help you check that you have everything you need.

Step-by-step
Step-by-step instructions tell you exactly what to do at each stage of a project.

Things to remember

- Read all the instructions and gather together everything you will need before you begin a project.

- Be very careful when using wire strippers, scissors, and screwdrivers. Do not use them unless an adult is there to help.

- Always turn off battery-powered projects when you are not using them since batteries may get hot or run down.

- For projects requiring electricity, always use batteries. Never use electricity from the wall sockets because it is very dangerous.

- When you have finished, put your project away safely and clean up everything you have used.

A DK PUBLISHING BOOK

Editor Sarah Johnston
Designer Caroline Potts and Adrienne Hutchinson
DTP Designer Almudena Díaz
Managing Editor Jane Yorke
Managing Art Editor Chris Scollen
US Editor Kristin Ward
Production Ben Smith
Photography Dave King
First American Edition, 1997
2 4 6 8 10 9 7 5 3 1
Published in the United States by DK Publishing, Inc,
95 Madison Avenue, New York, New York 10016.
Visit us on the World Wide Web at http://www.dk.com

Copyright © 1997 Dorling Kindersley Limited, London
Projects originally published in *My First Science Book*,
My First Photography Book and *My First Batteries and Magnets Book*,
Copyright © 1996, 1994, 1994 Dorling Kindersley Limited, London

A catalog record is available from the Library of Congress.

ISBN 0-7894-1558-5

Color reproduction by Colourscan
Printed and bound in Italy by L.E.G.O

CONTENTS

PINHOLE CAMERA 6

CAMERA OBSCURA   8

MAKING
CONNECTIONS   10

STOCK CARS   12

LIGHTING-UP TIME   14

MOTOR MANIA   16
FAN-TASTIC   18
ELECTROMAGNETS   20
BUSY BUZZER   22

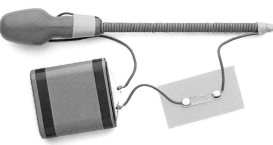

WEATHER STATION   24

WEATHER WATCH   26

MAKE IT MOVE   28

THE FINISHED
ZOETROPE   30

PINHOLE CAMERA

Make a pinhole in a lightproof box, put tracing paper on the opposite side, and instantly you have a simple camera! When light passes through the pinhole, it forms an image on the tracing paper. Find out how on the opposite page. If you used photographic paper (special paper that reacts to light) on the back of the box instead of tracing paper, a photograph would be produced. But, to see the image, you would need a darkroom and developing equipment.

Colored sticky tape

Tracing paper

Aluminum foil

Small cardboard box with a hinged lid

You will need

Strong glue

Poster paints

EQUIPMENT

Saucer

Jar of water

Paintbrush

Pencil

Needle or pin

Ruler

Scissors

Craft knife

Making the camera

1 Take the box apart and paint it. Paint the inside black. When paint's dry ask an adult to cut a large rectangle out of one side.

2 Ask an adult to cut a small square out of the side of the box opposite the rectangle. Glue the box back together. Let it dry.

3 Tape tracing paper over the large rectangular hole and foil over the square. Prick the center of the foil with a pin to make a hole.

The finished pinhole camera

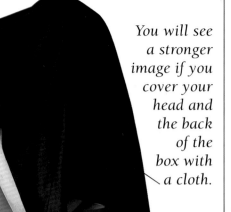

It is difficult to make a neat pinhole through cardboard. This is why a piece of aluminum foil is used.

Pinhole

Tape along the box edges. This gives a neat finish and stops light from getting inside.

The box must shut out the light.

Using the camera

Hold the box with the foil at the front.

Point the camera toward a window or an object in bright light. You will see an upside-down image on the tracing paper.

You will see a stronger image if you cover your head and the back of the box with a cloth.

HOW IS THE IMAGE FORMED?

Light travels in straight lines. Every object reflects some light. Here, light is reflected off the girl. It passes through the pinhole onto the tracing paper and forms a picture of the girl. If the pinhole is too big, the light will spread over a large area and form a blurred image.

The brighter the image, the easier it will be to see. Ask a friend to stand near a window so that he or she is brightly lit.

The farther away the object is from the pinhole, the smaller the image will be on the tracing paper.

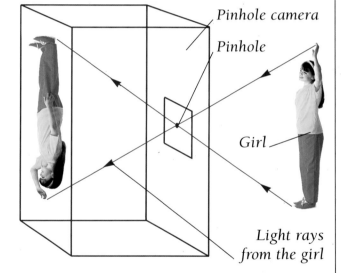

Pinhole camera

Pinhole

Girl

Light rays from the girl

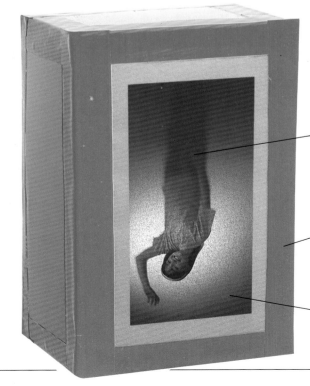

The image of the girl is upside down and reversed.

Pinhole camera

Tracing paper

WHY IS THE IMAGE UPSIDE DOWN?

The light coming from the girl's head passes through the pinhole in a downward direction to the bottom of the tracing paper. The light coming from the girl's feet passes through the pinhole in an upward direction to the top of the tracing paper. This happens to light from all over the girl, making the image upside down and reversed.

CAMERA OBSCURA

Instead of a pinhole, this camera uses a magnifying glass to form a picture on tracing paper. The glass works in a similar way to the lens on a "real" camera. It lets in more light than a pinhole, so it gives a brighter image.*

You will need

Poster board

Tracing paper

Small cardboard box with a hinged lid

Strong glue

Colored sticky tape

Poster paints

Small magnifying glass, with magnification of about x 2 (You can buy these from craft stores.)

Scissors

Jar of water

Pencil

Saucer

Paintbrush

Ruler

Craft knife

Making the camera

1 Gently take the box apart and paint it. Paint the inside black. Let the box dry. Ask an adult to cut a large rectangle out of one side.

2 Cut out a 4 x 8 in (10 x 20 cm) rectangle of poster board. Roll and tape it into a tube that fits the lens, as shown.

3 Hold the tube on the side of the box that is opposite the large rectangular hole. Trace around it with a pencil.

*Unlike the pinhole camera, this camera gives a sharp image with a large hole because the lens focuses the light.

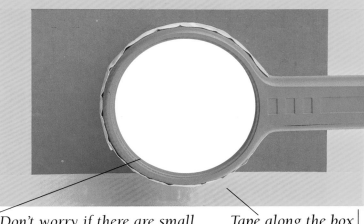

The finished camera obscura

The camera obscura was developed from the pinhole camera. Camera obscuras, similar to the one you have made, were used by artists more than 400 years ago to cast an image on to a wall or canvas, which they would then copy.

Don't worry if there are small gaps around the tube. The camera will still work.

Tape along the box edges to keep light from getting in.

4 Ask an adult to cut out the circle you have drawn with a craft knife. Glue the box back together and leave it to dry.

5 Cut a piece of tracing paper to fit over the rectangular hole on one side of the box. Tape the tracing paper over the hole.

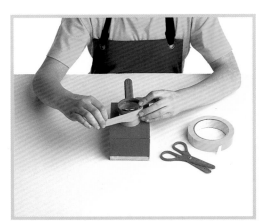

6 Slot the tube into its hole, as shown. You should be able to slide it in and out of the box. Tape the magnifying glass to the tube.

Focus by pushing the tube in or out.

Using the camera

Point the magnifying glass towards an object that is in bright light. Push the tube in or out of the box until you see the image focused (sharp) on the tracing paper.

HOW DOES IT WORK?

Light rays coming from the object pass through the magnifying glass. The glass bends the rays and makes them meet (or focus) on the tracing paper, where they form a picture.

CAMERA LENSES

Camera lenses are more complicated shapes than a magnifying glass and make even sharper pictures. Instead of tracing paper, there is light-sensitive film in a "real" camera. When you take a photograph, an image is formed on the light-sensitive film. The photograph is then developed and printed.

Just like the picture formed by the pinhole camera, the image on the tracing paper is upside down and reversed.

Camera obscura

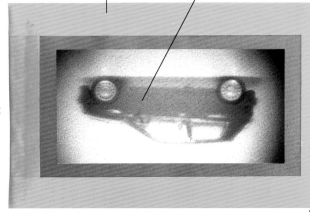

MAKING CONNECTIONS

Batteries can make things happen! They produce electricity, which can turn a motor or light a bulb. Before the electricity can flow, it must have a path from one side, or terminal, of the battery to the other. This path is called a circuit. On this page you will find out how to connect a battery in a circuit, to light a bulb. You can also make a switch to turn the bulb on and off.

You will need

Plastic-coated wire

A 4.5V battery

A 3.5V or 4.5V bulb

A bulb holder

Paper fasteners

A steel paper clip

Making a simple circuit

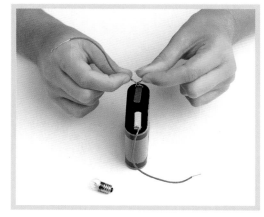

1 Cut two pieces of wire, and carefully strip about 1 in (2.5cm) of plastic from the ends. Twist bare metal strands together.

2 Twist a wire tightly around each of the battery terminals, as shown. Make sure that the bare wire is touching the terminal.

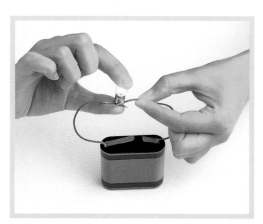

3 Touch one wire to the bottom of the bulb and one to its side. You have made a complete circuit, and the bulb will light up.

4 Screw the bulb into the bulb holder and attach the wires around the screws, as shown, using a screwdriver. The bulb is lit.

Corrugated cardboard

EQUIPMENT

Phillips-head screwdriver

Wire strippers　　*Scissors*

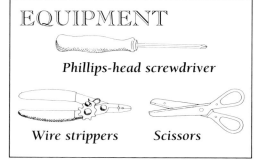

10

Making a switch

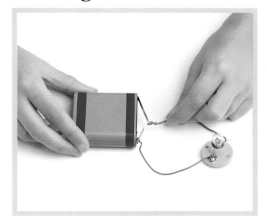

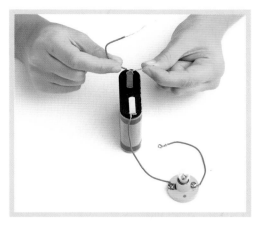

5 Take one of the wires off the battery. The bulb will go out because there is no longer a complete circuit.

6 Cut another piece of wire. Strip away 1 in (2.5 cm) of plastic from each end of the wire and twist the metal strands, as before.

7 Attach one end of the wire to the disconnected terminal of the battery. The other end of the wire will connect to the switch.

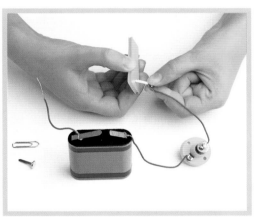

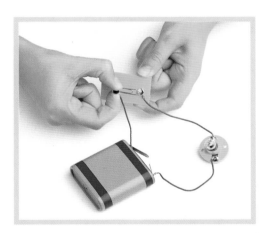

8 Carefully cut out a rectangle of cardboard, about 1½ x 2 in (3 x 5 cm). This base will hold the pieces you need for the switch.

9 Wind the end of the wire from the bulb holder firmly around a paper fastener and push the fastener through the cardboard.

10 Do the same with the end of the other wire, as shown, but this time put a paper clip around the paper fastener as well.

THE COMPLETED CIRCUIT

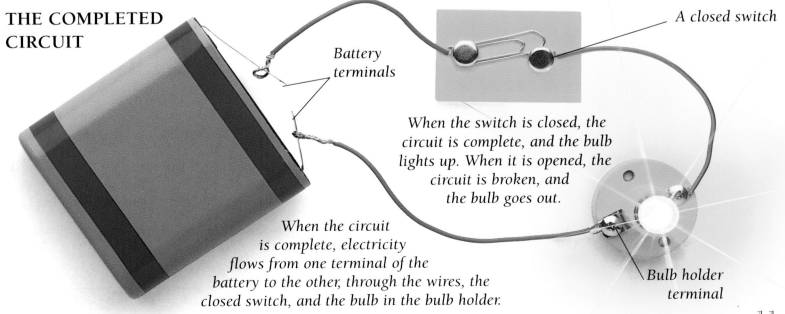

A closed switch

Battery terminals

When the switch is closed, the circuit is complete, and the bulb lights up. When it is opened, the circuit is broken, and the bulb goes out.

When the circuit is complete, electricity flows from one terminal of the battery to the other, through the wires, the closed switch, and the bulb in the bulb holder.

Bulb holder terminal

STOCK CARS

Did you know that a car's lights are powered by battery? The lights are connected in two different circuit types. Headlights are connected "in series" (the bulbs are wired together, one after the other, in a circuit). The indicators are connected "in parallel" (two separate circuits are connected to the same battery). Here you can find out how to make an electrifying stock car with working headlights and turn signals.

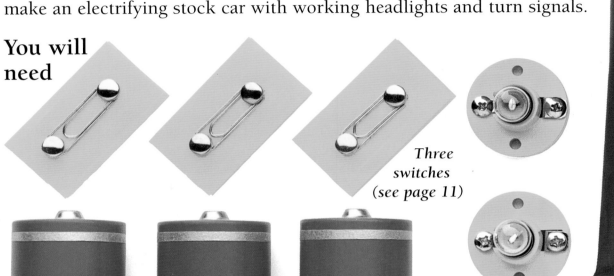

About 3 ft (1 m) of wire

You will need

Three switches (see page 11)

Four wooden skewers

Strong glue

Three 1.5V batteries

An egg carton

Four 1.5V bulbs in bulb holders

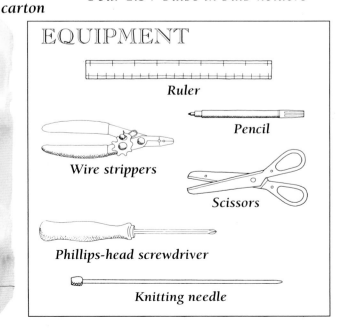

EQUIPMENT

Ruler

Pencil

Wire strippers

Scissors

Phillips-head screwdriver

Knitting needle

A shoe box, with its lid

Four model car wheels, or circles of stiff cardboard

Colored paper

Colored tape

Aluminum foil

Making the car body

1 Cut away the box, as shown, making sure that the long sides of the car are the same.* Tape the back flap to the sides of the car.

2 Cut the box lid to fit the top of the car and a windshield. Fold down the cut end to make the windshield. Then tape it in place.**

3 Push one wheel onto each pair of skewers. Make holes for axles: two holes at the rear of the car and two below the windshield.*

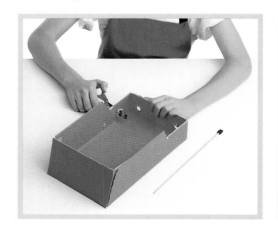

4 Make two holes, large enough for a bulb to go through, in the front of the car. Then, make a hole on each side of the hood.

5 Poke the skewers through the axle holes and push on the two remaining wheels. Decorate the stock car with colored paper.

6 Cover two egg carton cups with foil. Make a big hole in the bottom of each cup, then glue one over each headlight hole.

---

*Ask an adult to help you with this.   ***The piece of lid becomes the car's hood*

LIGHTING-UP TIME

Headlights "in series"

Turn signals "in parallel"

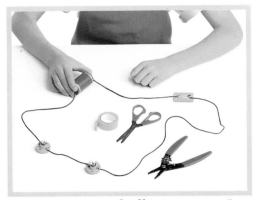

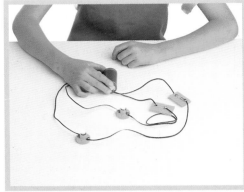

1 Connect two bulbs "in series" in a circuit. The lights are dim because one battery is too weak to power two bulbs wired "in series."

2 Tape the top of a battery to the bottom of another, "in series." Connect the batteries to the circuit, as shown. Now the lights are bright.

Connect two separate circuits, each with a bulb and a switch, to one battery, as shown. Bulbs wired "in parallel" shine brightly.

Stock car crash

The car headlights are wired in series because both lights need to be on at the same time. Turn signals are used one at a time, so they are wired in parallel, with separate switches.

Glue a large paper number to the roof, sides, and hood of your stock car.

BRIGHT LIGHTS!

Foil cups around the headlights reflect the light forward from the bulbs. This makes the headlights appear brighter.

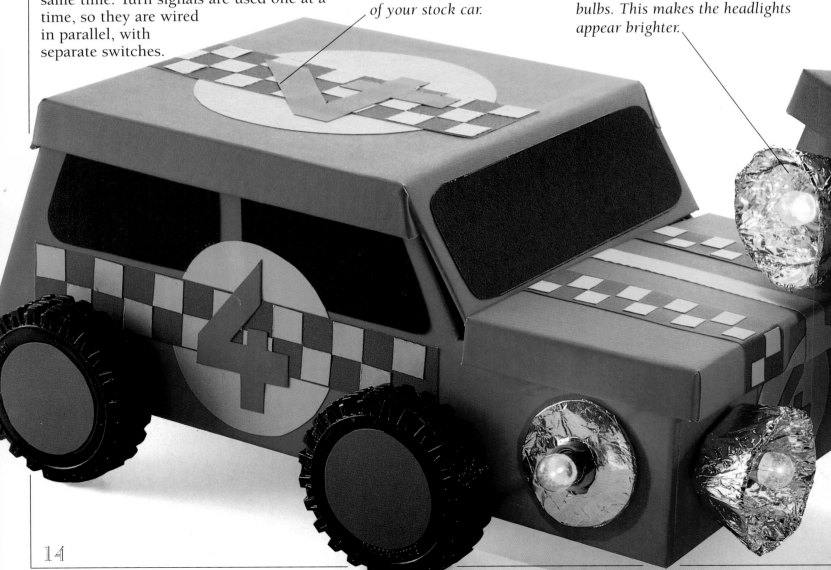

Attaching the lights

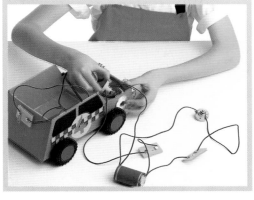

1 Put the headlights circuit into the car. Glue the switch to the back of the car. Push one bulb through each foil cup, as shown.

2 Cut two doughnut shapes out of cardboard. Cover with foil. Glue one over each side hole. Put a turn signal bulb through each hole.

3 Put the circuits in the car. Glue the left turn signal switch to the car's left side and the right turn signal switch to the right side.

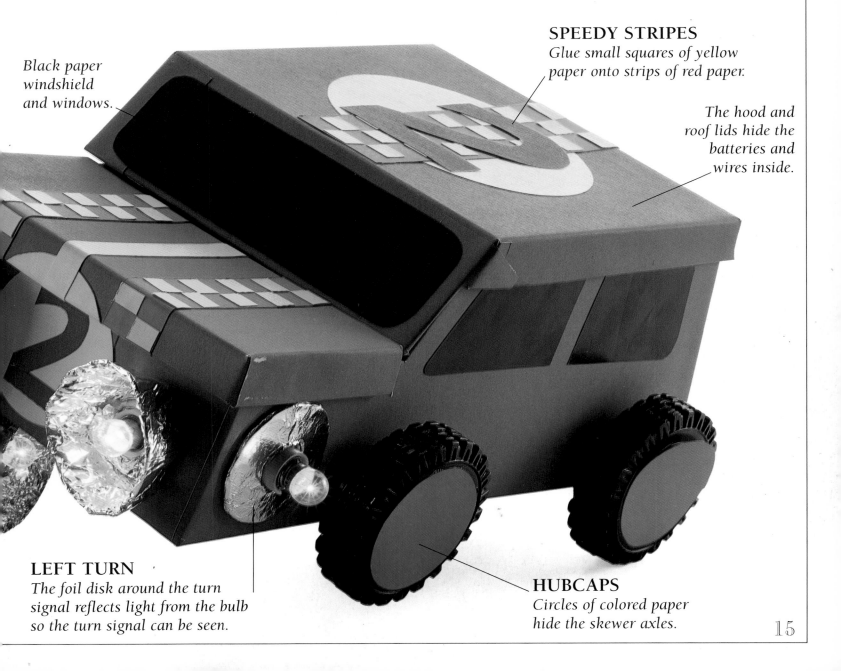

Black paper windshield and windows.

SPEEDY STRIPES
Glue small squares of yellow paper onto strips of red paper.

The hood and roof lids hide the batteries and wires inside.

LEFT TURN
The foil disk around the turn signal reflects light from the bulb so the turn signal can be seen.

HUBCAPS
Circles of colored paper hide the skewer axles.

15

MOTOR MANIA

Electricity can do a lot more than light bulbs. If you connect a battery to an electric motor, you can make things move, too! Here and on the next two pages you can find out how to make colorful fans to keep you cool, and a spectacular, whirling merry-go-round.

Plastic cotton swab

18 Pipe cleaners

Four thread spools

You will need

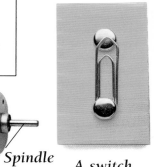

Pattern for the eagles

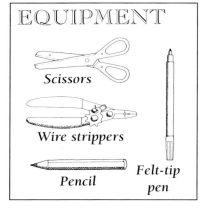

EQUIPMENT

Scissors

Wire strippers

Pencil

Felt-tip pen

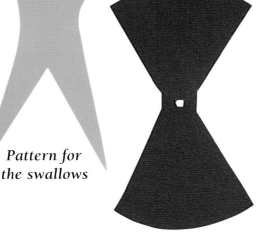

Pattern for the swallows

A switch (see page 11)

A 1.5V battery

Pattern for the fans

Motor terminals

Spindle

A 1.5V-4V electric motor

Connecting the motor

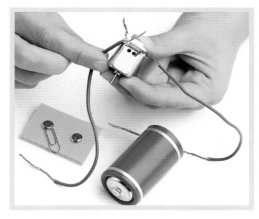

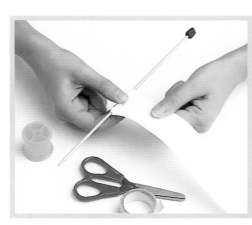

1 Connect a stripped wire to each terminal of the motor, as shown.* Cut a stem from a cotton swab. Push it onto the spindle.

2 Connect the motor in a circuit as shown. Glue the motor to the box, so that the top of the spindle is level with the top of the box.

3 To make a "sleeve," roll a strip of paper around the knitting needle. The sleeve must fit snugly into the center of one spool.

16   *Divide the end of the wire in half, thread one half through the terminal, then twist the two halves together.*

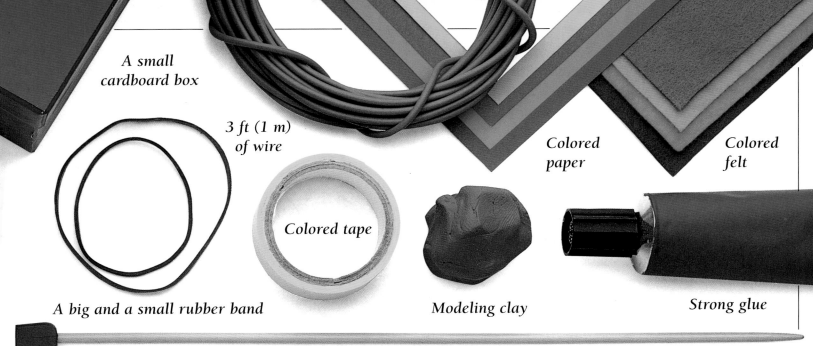

A small cardboard box

3 ft (1 m) of wire

Colored tape

Colored paper

Colored felt

A big and a small rubber band

Modeling clay

Strong glue

A knitting needle

Making the merry-go-round

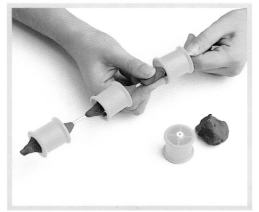

4 Stick the three other spools on the needle with the clay, as shown. Glue the spool with a sleeve to the bottom of the box.

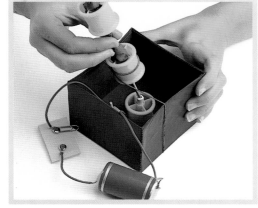

5 Stretch the big rubber band around the box. Put the small band around the third spool from the top of the needle, as shown.

6 Use three pipe cleaners for each bird – one for the head and body, and one for each wing. Bend head shapes as shown.

7 Trace the eagle and swallow patterns, then cut them out of felt. Make three of each. Tape birds to the pipe cleaner bodies.

8 Tape a pipe-cleaner to each bird. Tape all the birds to the top two spools, as shown. Stand the needle in the spool, in the box.

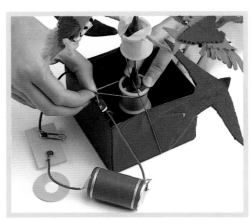

9 Stretch the small rubber band around the spindle. Adjust the banded spool so that its top is level with the top of the motor.**

**Adjust the bottom spool as necessary.

Fan-Tastic

Making a fan

1 Cut out a cardboard fan using pattern on page 16. Decorate it with colored paper, then make a hole in the middle with a pencil.

2 Connect a switch, motor, and battery together in a circuit. Push a tube cut from a cotton swab onto the motor's spindle.

3 Push the fan shape onto the spindle. Stick it in place with modeling clay. Bend cardboard, as shown, to make fan blades.

WHIRLING MERRY-GO-ROUND

Add the finishing touches to your merry-go-round by putting the battery in one corner of the box, where it won't be seen. Then, glue the switch to the outside, where you can turn it on and off easily.

Blue felt swallow

Pipe-cleaner supports

Pink, blue, and yellow felt eagle

Small rubber band

IN A SPIN

As the motor runs, the spindle turns very quickly, making the small rubber band stretched between the needle and the spindle move around too. This, in turn, makes the knitting needle and merry-go-round spin.

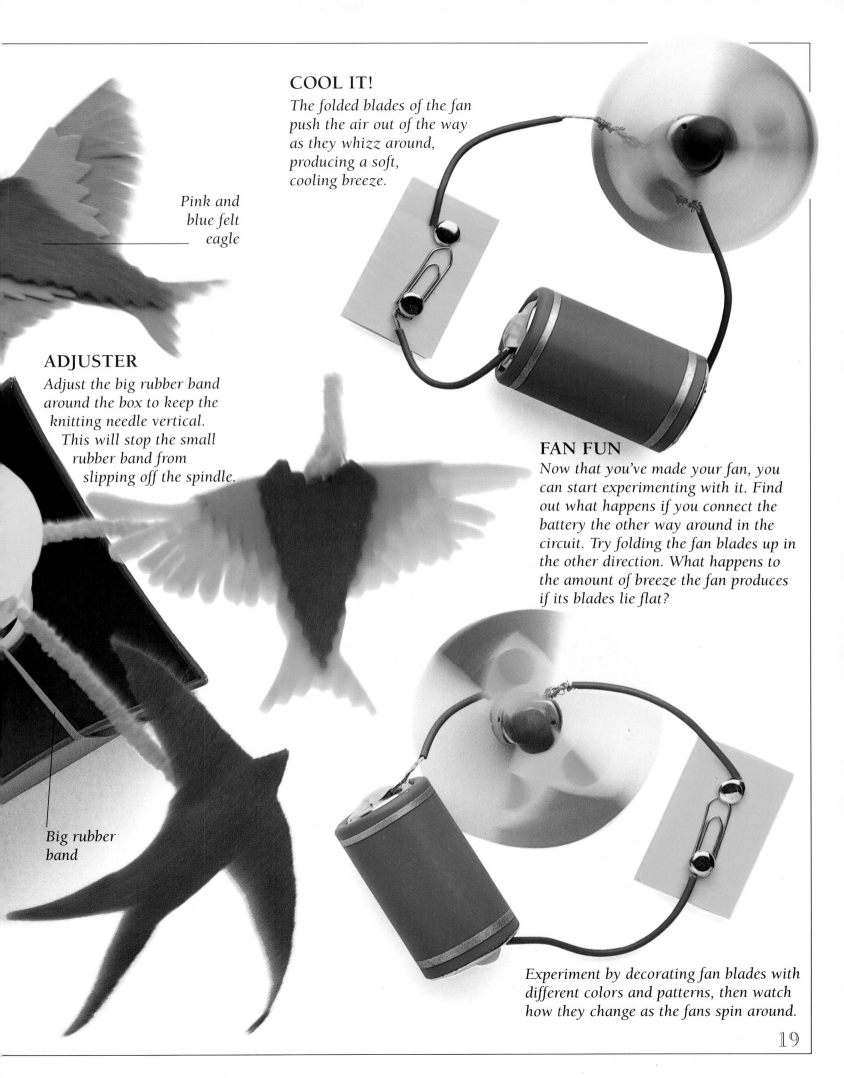

COOL IT!

The folded blades of the fan push the air out of the way as they whizz around, producing a soft, cooling breeze.

Pink and blue felt eagle

ADJUSTER

Adjust the big rubber band around the box to keep the knitting needle vertical. This will stop the small rubber band from slipping off the spindle.

Big rubber band

FAN FUN

Now that you've made your fan, you can start experimenting with it. Find out what happens if you connect the battery the other way around in the circuit. Try folding the fan blades up in the other direction. What happens to the amount of breeze the fan produces if its blades lie flat?

Experiment by decorating fan blades with different colors and patterns, then watch how they change as the fans spin around.

19

ELECTROMAGNETS

You can make magnets with electricity, too. They are called electromagnets and, unlike ordinary magnets, their magnetic powers can be switched on and off. All you need is a battery, some wire, a screwdriver, and a switch. The experiment works best if the screwdriver has an iron shaft, but a steel shaft will work.

Colored tape

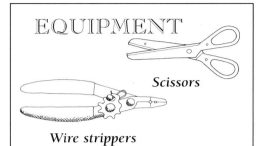

About 6 ft (2 m) of plastic-coated wire

You will need

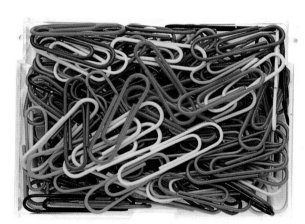

EQUIPMENT

Scissors

Wire strippers

A switch (see page 11)

A 4.5V battery

Lots of paper clips

A long screwdriver

What to do

1 Strip the ends of a long piece of wire. Tape one end to the handle of a screwdriver, leaving the other end of the wire free.

2 Wind the wire tightly around the screwdriver 20, 40, or 60 times. Tape the last turn of the wire firmly to the screwdriver.

3 Connect the switch, battery, and screwdriver in a circuit, as shown. How many paper clips can each electromagnet pick up?

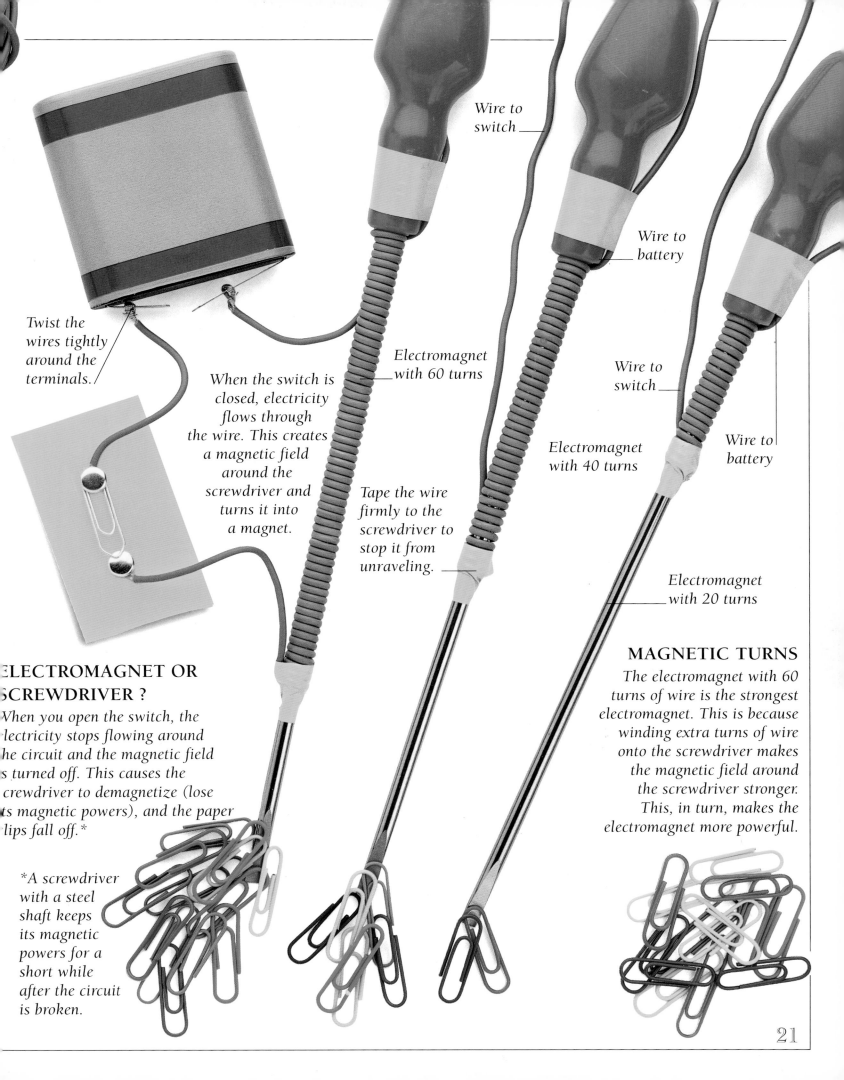

Twist the wires tightly around the terminals.

When the switch is closed, electricity flows through the wire. This creates a magnetic field around the screwdriver and turns it into a magnet.

Tape the wire firmly to the screwdriver to stop it from unraveling.

Wire to switch

Wire to battery

Electromagnet with 60 turns

Wire to switch

Wire to battery

Electromagnet with 40 turns

Electromagnet with 20 turns

ELECTROMAGNET OR SCREWDRIVER ?

When you open the switch, the electricity stops flowing around the circuit and the magnetic field is turned off. This causes the screwdriver to demagnetize (lose its magnetic powers), and the paper clips fall off.*

*A screwdriver with a steel shaft keeps its magnetic powers for a short while after the circuit is broken.

MAGNETIC TURNS

The electromagnet with 60 turns of wire is the strongest electromagnet. This is because winding extra turns of wire onto the screwdriver makes the magnetic field around the screwdriver stronger. This, in turn, makes the electromagnet more powerful.

21

BUSY BUZZER

You will need

Once you know how to make an electromagnet (see page 20), you can build this noisy buzzer. The handle of the nail file and the paint on the soda can don't conduct electricity, so make sure that wires are only connected to bare metal, or the buzzer won't work. As you follow the steps look at the photograph of the buzzer circuit to check that you have put everything in the right place.

A 4.5V battery

A metal soda can

A steel nail file

Corrugated cardboard

A switch (see page 11)

Modeling clay

A thread spool

A rubber band

Wire at least 10 ft (3 m) long

Colored tape

An iron or steel bolt

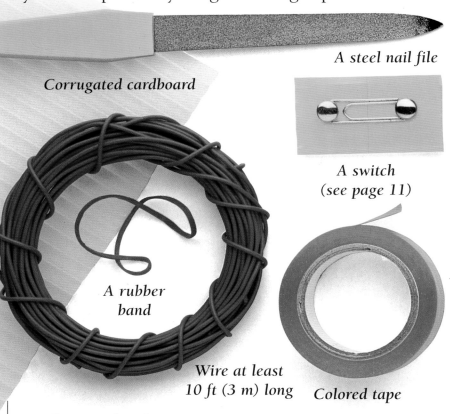

EQUIPMENT

Scissors

Wire strippers

Making the buzzer

1 Wrap the wire firmly around the bolt 200 times. Strip both ends of the wire. Stick the bolt to the cardboard with modeling clay.

2 Attach the nail file to the spool with the rubber band, as shown. Make sure that the nail file is held tightly in place.

3 Use the scissors to scratch away two squares of paint along the bottom edge on opposite sides of the soda can.

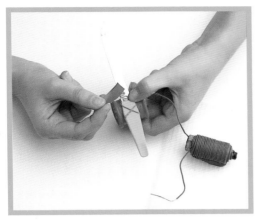

4 Firmly tape a wire from the bolt to the metal part of the nail file, as shown. Stick the spool in place on the cardboard with clay.

5 Cut a short piece of wire and strip its ends. Attach one end to the battery. Tape the other to one of the scratched squares on the can.

6 Stick can to cardboard with clay so the other square touches the nail file. Connect the bolt to a switch, then to the battery.

BUZZING ABOUT

When you close the switch, electricity flows around the circuit. The bolt becomes an electromagnet and pulls the nail file away from the can. This breaks the circuit, so that the electromagnet loses its power and the nail file springs back, hits the can, and completes the circuit again. This process happens over and over, very quickly.

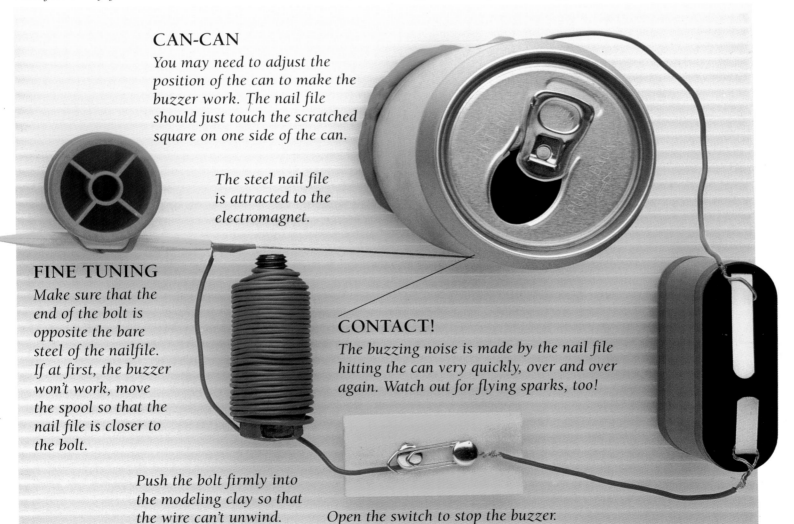

CAN-CAN

You may need to adjust the position of the can to make the buzzer work. The nail file should just touch the scratched square on one side of the can.

The steel nail file is attracted to the electromagnet.

FINE TUNING

Make sure that the end of the bolt is opposite the bare steel of the nailfile. If at first, the buzzer won't work, move the spool so that the nail file is closer to the bolt.

Push the bolt firmly into the modeling clay so that the wire can't unwind.

CONTACT!

The buzzing noise is made by the nail file hitting the can very quickly, over and over again. Watch out for flying sparks, too!

Open the switch to stop the buzzer.

WEATHER STATION

Set up your own weather station and you will be able to keep a record of your local weather. Here and on the following pages you can find out how to make a rain gauge for measuring rainfall; a barometer to show changes in air pressure; and a wind vane to show which way the wind is blowing.

You will need

Food coloring or ink

Waterproof tape

A glue stick

A short pencil with an eraser on the end
Three long pencils

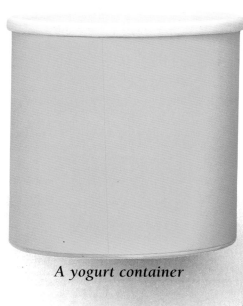

A drinking straw

A shallow bowl

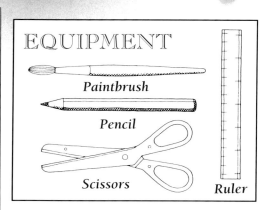

EQUIPMENT

Paintbrush

Pencil

Scissors

Ruler

A yogurt container

A large plastic bottle

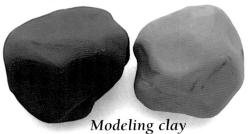

Thin cardboard

A thumbtack

Modeling clay

A narrow, clear plastic bottle*

Making the wind vane

1 Make a hole in the center of the base of the yogurt container. Push short pencil into it, leaving the eraser end sticking out.

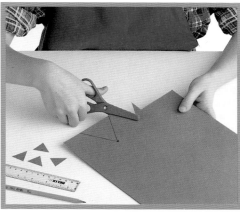

2 Cut four small triangles out of cardboard. **Then cut one triangle about 1¼ in (3 cm) deep and a bigger one 2 in (5 cm) deep.

3 Glue the four small triangles to the base of the yogurt container, so that they point in four different directions, as shown.

4 Cut a ½ in (1 cm) slit at each end of the straw. Slot a big triangle into each slit, both pointing in the same direction.

5 Push the thumbtack through the center of the straw and into the eraser. Make sure the vane can spin easily.

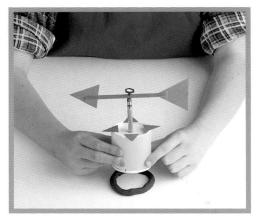

6 Roll up some modeling clay and bend it into a circle. Push the clay around the base of the wind vane.

*Use the narrowest bottle you can find.   ***Ask an adult to help you.*   25

WEATHER WATCH

Making the rain gauge

1 Cut off the top quarter of the large plastic bottle, using the scissors. Ask an adult to help you.

2 Slide the top of the bottle upside down into the base of the bottle, to act as a funnel. Tape the edges together, as shown.

3 Cut tiny strips of waterproof tape. Tape them to the side of the bottle about 1/4 in (1 cm) apart. This will be your measuring scale.

Making the barometer

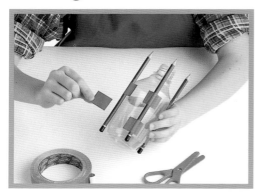

1 Tape three long pencils to the small plastic bottle. The points of the pencils should stick out above the top of the bottle.

2 Using the bottle as a guide, stick three lumps of modeling clay to the bottom of the bowl. The pencils will go into them.

3 Half fill both the bowl and the bottle with water. With the paintbrush, add a few drops of food coloring or ink to the water.

4 Cover the top of the bottle with your hand. Turn it upside down and lower it under the water in the bowl.

5 Take your hand away from the mouth of the bottle. Keeping the bottle straight, push the pencils firmly into the modeling clay.

6 Cut tiny strips of tape. Tape them to the side of the bottle to make a scale as on the rain gauge.

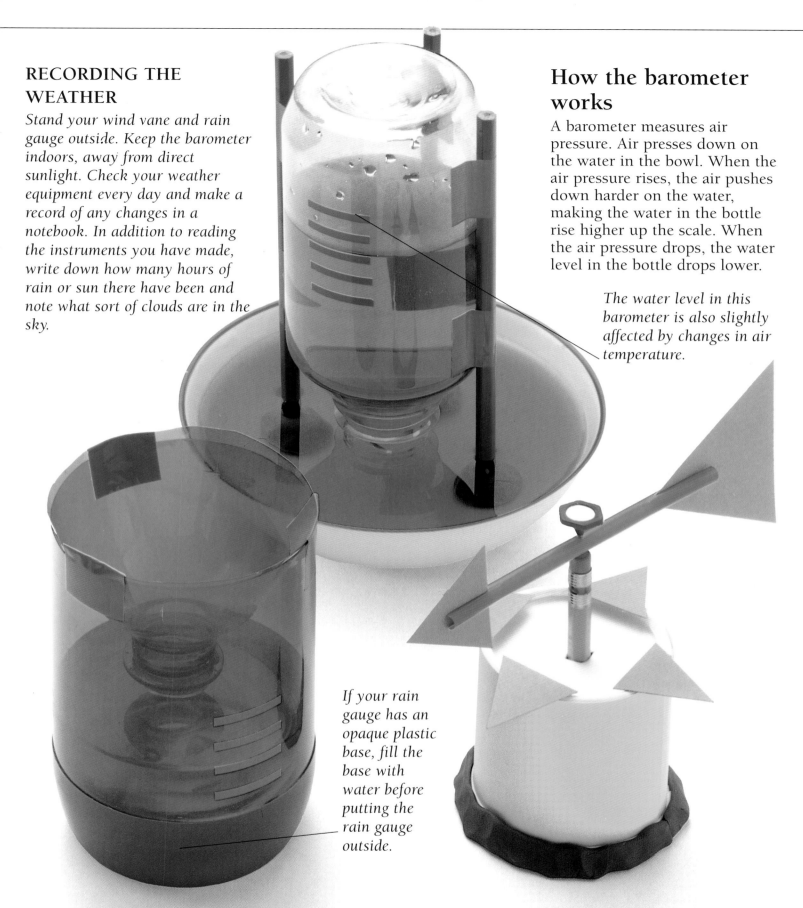

RECORDING THE WEATHER

Stand your wind vane and rain gauge outside. Keep the barometer indoors, away from direct sunlight. Check your weather equipment every day and make a record of any changes in a notebook. In addition to reading the instruments you have made, write down how many hours of rain or sun there have been and note what sort of clouds are in the sky.

How the barometer works

A barometer measures air pressure. Air presses down on the water in the bowl. When the air pressure rises, the air pushes down harder on the water, making the water in the bottle rise higher up the scale. When the air pressure drops, the water level in the bottle drops lower.

The water level in this barometer is also slightly affected by changes in air temperature.

If your rain gauge has an opaque plastic base, fill the base with water before putting the rain gauge outside.

Measuring the rainfall

When it rains, check how far up the scale the water comes every day. Make a note of the reading, then empty the rain gauge.

Which way is the wind blowing?

Stand the wind vane outside on a flat surface. Use a compass to position it so that one of the triangles points north. Mark the triangles north, south, east, and west. Write down which direction the wind is blowing from. A north wind, for example, blows from north to south.

27

MAKE IT MOVE!

When you look at a sequence of action photographs passing quickly before your eyes, the images look as if they are moving, just like a movie at a theater. You can see this effect by looking into a machine called a zoetrope. Before you make the zoetrope, you will need to take 13 photographs showing someone doing each stage of a simple action. Below, photographs of a clown lifting his hat and then putting it back on are used.

Colored poster board

You will need

A sequence of 13 action photographs taken on a plain background

Jar lid

Medium-sized beads

Two empty thread spools

Strong glue

Pencil

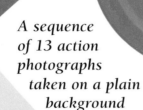

Colored tape

Making the zoetrope

1 Use compass to draw a circle with a radius of 5 in (12.5 cm) on poster board. Cut it out. Draw around thread spool in the center.

2 Ask an adult to cut slightly within the thread spool circle, making a hole that the spool fits into without sliding out.

3 Glue one thread spool onto the inside of a jar lid and one to the outside. Glue a pencil into the spool on the outside of the lid.

4 Cut a strip of board 4½ x 32 in (11.5 x 81 cm).* Measure ¼ in (0.5 cm) wide slots every 2⅛ in (5.5 cm). Mark along one edge.

5 Mark each of the ¼ in (0.5 cm) wide slots to be 1½ in (4 cm) deep. Use a ruler to draw the slots neatly. Cut them out.

6 Overlap the ends of the slotted poster board by ⅝ in (2 cm) and glue to make a tube. Tape the circle of poster board, as shown

7 Trim prints into small rectangles. Stick onto poster board 3 x 31½ in (7.5 x 80 cm)**. Leave a ⅝ in (2 cm) gap one end.

8 Overlap the strip by ⅝ in(2 cm and glue it to make a tube with the prints on the inside. Put it in the drum, and beads in the jar lid.

9 Push the spool through the hole in the base of the drum. It should fit snugly. The zoetrope is now ready to spin!

*Stick two strips of poster board together to make it stronger.

**Stick down cutout prints 2 ⅛ in (6 cm) in order to make an action sequence.

THE FINISHED ZOETROPE

When you spin the drum and look through the slits, the pictures will appear to move! The drum spins on the loose beads in the jar lid. Try making several action sequences to place inside your zoetrope. You and your friends will have lots of fun seeing each other in action.

THE ZOETROPE PHOTOGRAPHS

Ask a friend to wear bright colors that will show up well and to stand against a plain background. The plain background will help you join the photographs together easily. Take the photographs outside on a sunny day or use your camera's flash indoors.

When you glue your action photographs onto poster board, leave a thin border at the top and bottom. This will help your photographs stand out.

Blue and yellow sheets of poster board were stuck together to make this zoetrope. Using two sheets makes the drum stronger.

A SIMPLE ACTION

Keep your action shots simple. Someone waving, clapping, or taking off a hat, as shown here, is easy to catch on film. Get a friend to do the action very slowly and to stop at each stage so that you can take a photograph of each small move. Remember to sort the action photographs into the correct order when you get the prints.

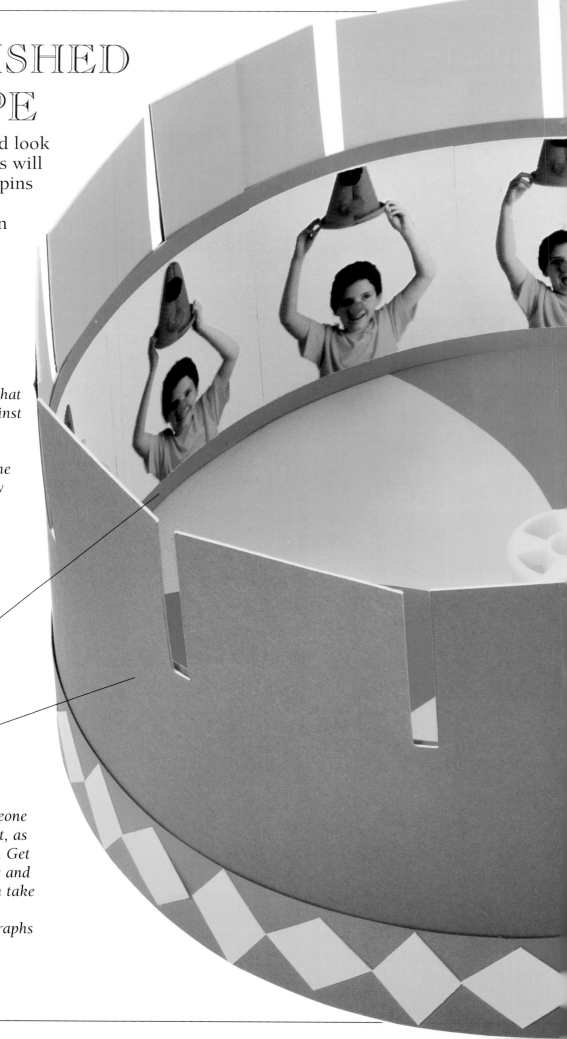

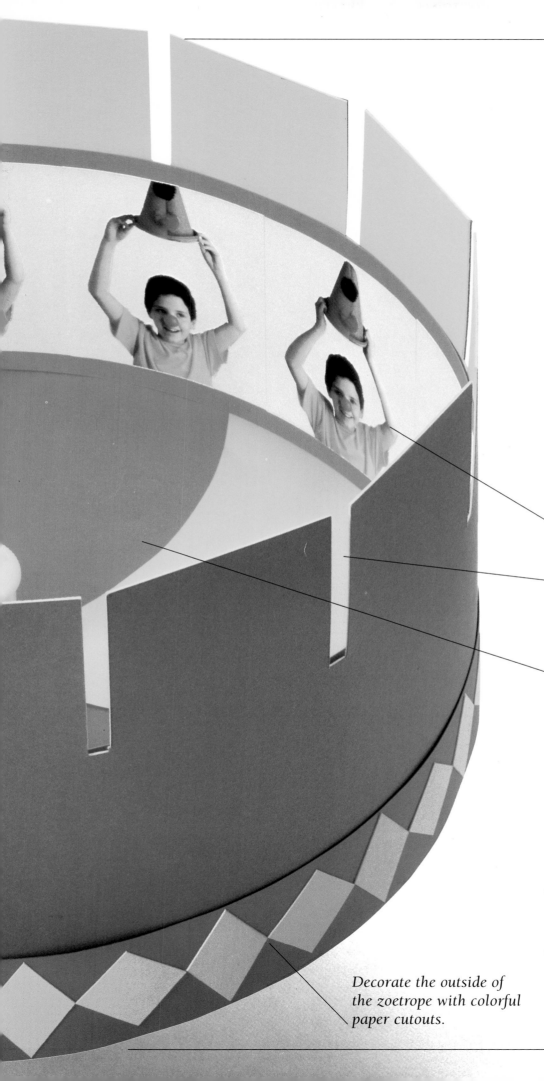

Using the zoetrope

Hold the pencil so that the drum is at your eye level. Spin the zoetrope. Look at the photographs through the slits in the drum. Hold the zoetrope carefully so you don't spill the beads.

Don't worry if your photographs overlap a little at the join of the tube. You should still see moving pictures.

The slots are 2⅛ in (5.5 cm) apart, ¼ in (0.5 cm) wide, and 1½ in (4 cm) deep.

You can decorate the base of the drum with paper shapes.

BEAD BEARINGS

The beads in the jar lid are not glued in. They are loose so that the drum can spin around on them.

HOW DOES IT WORK?

As each slot in the zoetrope passes in front of your eye, you see each picture for a fraction of a second. Your brain holds one image before the next comes into view, so that the pictures merge. When the drum spins fast, the pictures blend together and seem to move. Movie film works in the same way.

Decorate the outside of the zoetrope with colorful paper cutouts.

31